TABLE OF CONTENTS

Water Everywhere 4

Water Is Important 10

Drinking Enough............ 18

Staying Safe 24

Glossary 30

Read More 31

Internet Sites 31

Index 32

About the Author 32

Words in **bold** are defined in the glossary.

WATER EVERYWHERE

You wake up and drink from a glass on your night table. Maybe you have juice at breakfast. You sip from a sports bottle during school. Then you end the day with a cup of tea.

Healthy Foods

WATER
Is Good for You!

by
Gloria Koster

PEBBLE
a capstone imprint

Published by Pebble, an imprint of Capstone.
1710 Roe Crest Drive,
North Mankato, Minnesota 56003
capstonepub.com

Library of Congress Cataloging-in-Publication Data
Names: Koster, Gloria, author.
Title: Water is good for you! / by Gloria Koster.
Description: North Mankato, Minnesota : Pebble, [2023] | Series: Healthy foods | Includes bibliographical references and index. | Audience: Ages 5-8 | Audience: Grades K-1 | Summary: "From a tall glass of ice water to a steaming cup of tea, water is an essential part of any healthy diet. In this Pebble Explore book, learn more about where water comes from, the best sources of water, and how this drink helps make up a healthy diet. Filled with fantastic facts and colorful photos, this book will quench every young learner's thirst for knowledge"-- Provided by publisher.
Identifiers: LCCN 2022008220 (print) | LCCN 2022008221 (ebook) |
    ISBN 9781666351293 (hardcover) | ISBN 9781666351354 (paperback) |
    ISBN 9781666351415 (pdf) | ISBN 9781666351538 (kindle edition)
Subjects: LCSH: Water in the body--Juvenile literature. | Drinking water--Health aspects--Juvenile literature.
Classification: LCC QP535.H1 K67 2023 (print) | LCC QP535.H1 (ebook) | DDC 613.2/87--dc23/eng/20220602
LC record available at https://lccn.loc.gov/2022008220
LC ebook record available at https://lccn.loc.gov/2022008221

Editorial Credits
Editor: Donald Lemke; Designer: Tracy Davies; Media Researcher: Julie De Adder; Production Specialist: Katy LaVigne

Image Credits
Getty Images: AndreiDavid, 27, Bim, 8, Christopher Bernard, 28, FatCamera, 14, 23, Images By Tang Ming Tung, 18, Imgorthand, 19, kate_sept2004, 15, Klaus Vedfelt, 11, Science Photo Library, 16, SolStock, 26, Tashi-Delek, 4, Triolo Productions/Burke, 29; Shutterstock: Aleksandra Dabrowa, 10, atsurkan, 20, Digital Media Pro, 12, Fafarumba (water doodles), cover and throughout, fizkes, 13, Hatchapong Palurtchaivong, 21, Iraida Bearlala (background), cover and throughout, Katiekk, 24, Littlekidmoment, cover (front), 17, narikin, 7, NKneidlphoto, 5, Noel V. Baebler, 25, sonsart, 6, Stock video footage, 9

You are getting a lot of water!

Water is a **liquid**. It is important to all life on Earth.

Turn on a **faucet**. Fill up a glass with water. How does the water get there?

Clouds are full of water droplets. These droplets fall to Earth. In warm weather, they fall as rain. They come down as snow in cold weather.

Rain and snow fill the oceans. They fill lakes and rivers. Water goes into the ground too.

Do you live in a town or city?

Your water may start at a lake or river. It is cleaned at a **treatment** center. It travels through pipes. Then the water arrives at your home.

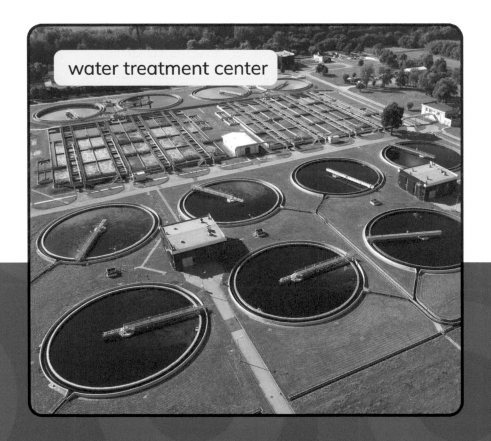

water treatment center

water well with pump

Do you live in the country?

You may have a **well**. Your water comes from deep in the ground. A pump brings the water to the surface.

WATER IS IMPORTANT

People need drinking water to stay alive. Animals and plants do too.

Humans can go more than a week without eating food. They can live only a few days without water.

Water does many jobs in your body. **Plasma** is the watery part of your blood. Plasma carries **nutrients** to your cells.

The **saliva** in your mouth is mostly water. It helps you chew and swallow. It helps keep your teeth healthy too.

Water keeps you healthy in other ways. It is good for your skin. Water also helps your body stay at the right temperature.

How much do you weigh? More than half your weight is water!

But every day your body loses water. You sweat playing sports. You lose water going to the bathroom.

Losing some water is normal. Just remember to replace it! You can do this by drinking plain water.

Watermelon has a lot of water.

Your body gets water from other kinds of drinks and even food. Milk and fruit juices have water. Some fruits and vegetables contain a lot of water too!

Drinking plain water between meals is smart. But some people drink sweet drinks instead. They include chocolate milk, soda, or sports drinks.

These types of drinks have a lot of sugar. Don't drink them too often.

DRINKING ENOUGH

How much water should you drink?
Everyone is different. The amount
depends on your age and size.
It depends on how much you move.

The amount of water you need can also depend on the weather. On hot summer days, you may need to drink more. You may drink less on cooler days.

Drinking too little can make you **dehydrated**. This happens when you lose more water than you add.

How can you tell if you're drinking enough? First, listen to your thirst! If you're thirsty, you should drink more.

You can also check the color of your **urine**. Dark yellow often means you should drink more. Lighter yellow is better. Your body is **hydrated**.

You drink water in different ways. You drink it in different places.

Turn on the faucet at home. Sip water from the fountain at school. Buy bottled water at the grocery store.

Keeping water nearby is important. Do you play sports? Do you like biking or hiking with your family? Don't forget to take a bottle along!

STAYING SAFE

Many people have clean drinking water. But some parts of the world do not have enough fresh water. Their water may be unsafe.

Women collect water from a stream in Africa.

A sign warns that water is unsafe to drink.

Unsafe water may contain waste from farm animals. It could have garbage or **chemicals** in it. The water may have **bacteria** or **viruses**. These things can make you sick.

Water that comes from a faucet is usually clean and safe. Workers test it often. They may warn your town or city if it becomes unsafe.

If you go camping, you should make sure the water is safe to drink. It may look clean when it is not.

Water that is not clean to drink is unsafe for brushing teeth. It is unsafe for washing dishes. An adult must boil unsafe water before using it.

We use water in many ways. We
wash with it. We brush our teeth with
it. And most important, we drink it!

Drinking enough water every day can help keep you healthy. It can help you play, learn, and grow! It's a big part of a healthy diet.

GLOSSARY

bacteria (bak-TEER-ee-uh)—tiny living things that are all around you and inside you

chemical (KEM-uh-kuhl)—a substance used in chemistry, which is often dangerous

dehydrated (dee-HYE-dray-tid)—not having enough water in your body

faucet (FAW-sit)—a device with a valve used to turn the flow of water on and off

hydrated (HYE-dray-tid)—having plenty of water

liquid (LIK-qwid)—a wet substance that you can pour

nutrient (NOO-tree-uhnt)—the part of food that is needed for growth and health

plasma (PLAZ-muh)—clear, yellow, liquid part of blood

saliva (suh-LYE-vuh)—liquid that keeps your mouth moist

treatment (TREET-muhnt)—a process in which a chemical or other substance is put in something in order to clean it

urine (YUHR-in)— waste liquid that collects in the bladder before leaving the body

virus (VYE-ruhss)—a small particle that causes a disease and that spreads from one person or animal to another

well (WEHL)—a deep hole made in the ground through which water can be removed

READ MORE

Carlson-Berne, Emma. *Let's Explore the Water Cycle.* Minneapolis: Lerner Publications, 2021.

Schuh, Mari. *Food Is Fuel.* North Mankato, MN: Capstone, 2021.

Webster, Christy. *Follow That Food!* New York: Random House, 2021.

INTERNET SITES

Britannica Kids: "Water"
https://kids.britannica.com/kids/article/water/390625

Drop In the Bucket: "The Water Crisis"
https://dropinthebucket.org/water-facts/

Kids Health: Why Drinking Water Is the Way to Go
kidshealth.org/en/kids/water.html

INDEX

animals, 10, 25

blood, 12

dehydrated, 20–21

food, 10, 16–17

juice, 4, 16

milk, 16–17

rain, 7, 29

safety, 24–27, 29

saliva, 12

skin, 13

soda, 17

sports, 4, 14, 17, 22

sports drinks, 17

tea, 4

teeth, 12, 27, 28

urine, 21

water treatment center, 8

well, 9

ABOUT THE AUTHOR

A public and school librarian, Gloria Koster belongs to the Children's Book Committee of Bank Street College of Education. She enjoys both city and country life, dividing her time between Manhattan and the small town of Pound Ridge, New York. Gloria has three adult children and a bunch of energetic grandkids.